The Cold War

David Taylor

Heinemann Library
Chicago, Illinois

© 2001 Reed Educational & Professional Publishing
Published by Heinemann Library,
an imprint of Reed Educational & Professional Publishing,
Chicago, IL

Customer Service 888-454-2279

Visit our website at www.heinemannlibrary.com

Designed by AMR
Illustrated by Adrian Barclay and Art Construction
Originated by Dot Gradations
Printed by Wing King Tong in Hong Kong

05 04 03 02 01
10 9 8 7 6 5 4 3 2 1

Library of Congress Cataloging-in-Publication Data
Taylor, David.
   The Cold War / David Taylor.
      p. cm. -- (20th century perspectives)
   Includes bibliographical references and index.
   ISBN 1-57572-434-0 (lib. bdg.)   ISBN 1-58810-373-0 (pbk. bdg.)
1. Cold war--Juvenile literature. 2. World politics--1945-1989--Juvenile literature. [1. Cold war.
2. World politics--1945-1989.] I. Title. II. Series.

D843 .T34 2001
909.82'5--dc21

                                                                                    00-
063458

Acknowledgments
The publisher is grateful to the following for permission to reproduce copyright material:
Bettman/Corbis, p. 16; Corbis, pp. 13, 15, 17, 21, 23, 24, 26, 28, 29, 32, 33, 34, 37, 39, 40;
Corbis/Bettman, p. 6; Corbis/Nasa/Roger Resmeyer, p. 35; Hulton Getty, pp. 19, 31; Popperfoto,
pp. 9, 20, 41; REX, pp. 36, 38, 42; The Art Archive, p. 7

Cover photograph: AKG/Gardi

Special thanks to Christopher Gibb for his comments in the preparation of this book.

Some words are shown in bold, **like this.** You can find out what they mean by looking in the glossary.

Contents

What Was the Cold War?

The United States (U.S.) and the **Union of Soviet Socialist Republics (USSR)** came out of World War II in 1945 as **superpowers.** They were by far the two strongest countries in the world. Although they had fought together against **Nazi** Germany, they soon fell out after the war and became hostile rivals.

THE TWO SIDES IN THE COLD WAR

	The West	The East
SUPERPOWERS:	THE UNITED STATES	THE USSR
THEIR ALLIES:	WESTERN EUROPE	EASTERN EUROPE
	IN 1949 THE WEST FORMED AN ALLIANCE OF COUNTRIES CALLED THE NORTH ATLANTIC TREATY ORGANIZATION (NATO).	IN 1955 THE EAST FORMED AN ALLIANCE CALLED THE WARSAW PACT.

Between 1945 and 1989, the two countries and their **allies** were involved in a bitter conflict known as the "Cold War." Like two friends who had argued, the two sides cold-shouldered each other. Periodically, there were confrontations, but the United States and the USSR never used weapons directly against each other. That would have been far too dangerous, as both countries had huge stocks of hazardous nuclear weapons. So, if they did not use weapons against each other, how was the Cold War fought? The diagram below sums up how the Cold War was carried out.

This shows how the West and East fought each other during the Cold War.

U.S.

USSR

SPYING
CIA (U.S.)   KGB (USSR)

INFORMATION
Both sides used television, radio, films, and the press to get across their own point of view.

PROXY WARS
Example: The Arab-Israeli conflict

U.S. supported Israel in the Arab-Israeli conflict by providing money and weapons.

USSR supported the Arabs.

NUCLEAR ARMS RACE
Cruise missile (U.S.)

SS-18 missile (USSR)

PRESTIGE
Each side tried to gain prestige by beating the other at sport, e.g. by winning more medals at the Olympic Games

Munich 1972 Olga Korbut, gymnast (USSR) Mark Spitz, swimmer (U.S.)

We disagree

We believe in democracy

SPACE RACE
Moon landing (U.S.)   Soyuz (USSR)

STRONG WORDS AND THREATS
Carter (U.S.)   Brezhnev (USSR)

This illustrates the main differences between the democratic, capitalist West and the communist East.

Two different types of government

Both sides had a deep mistrust of each other because they believed in different types of government. The countries of the East were run by **communist** governments, whereas the countries of the West had **democratic, capitalist** governments. Both sides thought that their system was the correct one.

The Western countries hated communism and believed that the USSR was out to spread it throughout the world. They, therefore, did everything they could to stop it from spreading. The USSR always denied that it wanted to spread communism and said that the democratic countries were the ones who wanted to dominate the world.

This mistrust made the East and West highly suspicious of each other. Although no shots were fired directly between the two sides, the Cold War hung like a black cloud over the world for about 44 years. People everywhere lived with the fear that a nuclear war could break out at almost any time. When the Cold War came to a sudden and abrupt end in 1989, there was a huge sense of relief.

How Did the Cold War Start?

In 1917, the **Bolshevik Party** took control of Russia and turned it into a **communist** country. Under communism, the Bolsheviks believed that industry would be modernized and the people would have a better standard of living. During the **Russian Civil War** (1918–21), troops from the United States, Britain, Japan, and France were sent to Russia to try and overthrow the new government. They failed and, in 1923, Russia joined with three neighboring areas under Bolshevik control to form the **Union of Soviet Socialist Republics (USSR)**.

In 1941, during World War II, **Nazi** Germany invaded the USSR. The United States, Britain, and the USSR formed the "Grand Alliance" and fought together against Nazi Germany. Even so, distrust was just beneath the surface. Stalin wanted the United States and Britain to open up a **second front** against the Germans in France. They did not do this until 1944. Stalin believed that they had delayed it on purpose to give the Germans the time to inflict heavy losses on the **Red Army.**

The Yalta Conference

By the beginning of 1945, Germany was on the verge of defeat. Soviet troops had pushed the Germans back through Eastern Europe and were closing in on Berlin. From the west, the Americans and British were invading Germany. In February, Stalin, U.S. President Franklin Roosevelt, and Winston Churchill, the British prime minister, met at Yalta on the Black Sea to discuss what would happen at the end of the war. The "big three" decided the following:

1. Each country in Eastern Europe liberated from the Germans by the Red Army would hold free elections.
2. The **United Nations (UN)** Organization would be formed, to stop future wars.
3. When Germany was beaten, the USSR would enter the war against Japan.
4. Germany was to be divided into four zones: Britain, France, the United States, and the USSR would each occupy a zone. As Berlin, the capital, would be in the Soviet zone, it too would be divided into four sectors, with each country taking control of one sector.

The three leaders of the Grand Alliance at the Yalta Conference. From left to right: Stalin, Roosevelt, and Churchill.

Josef Stalin: a ruthless dictator (1879–1953)

The son of a shoemaker, Stalin joined the Bolshevik Party in 1903, and took part in the **Russian Revolution** in 1917. By 1928, he had become leader of the USSR, and within ten years had turned it into a powerful industrial nation. However, his policies were unpopular with many people. In the 1930s, people who opposed Stalin were arrested and put on trial. An estimated eighteen million people were sent to labor camps, half of whom were executed. Stalin was a ruthless dictator who kept a firm grip on the USSR.

The Potsdam Conference

On July 17, 1945, the wartime **allies** met again at Potsdam, outside Berlin. Two of the leaders had changed since Yalta. Clement Attlee was now British prime minister and President Harry S. Truman replaced Roosevelt, who had died on April 12. The three leaders decided to go ahead with the division of Germany and to put the Nazi leaders on trial for war crimes.

There was an uneasy atmosphere at the conference. Truman did not trust Stalin. He was worried because the Soviets had not held any free elections in Eastern Europe. What was Stalin up to? On the other hand, Stalin was alarmed when Truman told him that the United States had exploded the world's first atomic bomb just a day before the conference opened. Stalin was worried that the United States might also use this weapon against the USSR.

Events in Japan

The Americans did not need Soviet help to defeat Japan. On August 6 and 9, atomic bombs were dropped by the United States on the Japanese cities of Hiroshima and Nagasaki. On September 2, the Japanese signed the terms of surrender on board the *USS Missouri*. The United States was to occupy Japan. It helped to turn Japan into a democratic, independent country. In the years that followed, the U.S. pumped over two billion dollars into Japan so it could rebuild its economy. Meanwhile, in Europe, the seeds of the Cold War had already been sown.

The ruins of Hiroshima after it was hit by an atomic bomb on August 6, 1945.

The Iron Curtain Descends

The **USSR** had suffered badly in World War II. Over 27 million Soviet citizens died and 32,000 factories lay in ruins. Stalin did not want the USSR ever to be invaded again from the west, as it had been by **Nazi** Germany in 1941. He was determined to have friendly countries bordering the USSR. He ordered the **Red Army** to stay in Eastern Europe and put **communist** governments in power in each country. Soon Poland, Romania, Bulgaria, Hungary, Albania, and Czechoslovakia all had communist governments that were willing to take orders from Stalin. Each country became a Soviet **satellite.** Western leaders had hoped that Stalin would hold free elections in each country.

Below is Europe in 1949. Eastern European countries built large barbed-wire fences along their borders with the West.

Key
- The Iron Curtain
- → Advance of the Red Army 1944–45
- Communist countries
- Communist but not under control of USSR
- Capitalist democratic countries

NB: Austria was occupied by the U.S., USSR, Britain, and France until 1955 when it became independent.

N W E S

NORWAY

SWEDEN

Moscow •

North Sea

DENMARK

Baltic Sea

BRITAIN

NETH.

BELGIUM

LUX.

FRANCE

WEST GERMANY

SWITZERLAND

EAST GERMANY

Berlin

Stettin

POLAND

UNION OF SOVIET SOCIALIST REPUBLICS (USSR)

CZECHOSLOVAKIA

AUSTRIA

HUNGARY

Trieste

YUGOSLAVIA

ROMANIA

Black Sea

ITALY

BULGARIA

ALBANIA

GREECE

TURKEY

0   250 km
0   125 miles

Mediterranean Sea

They felt deceived and thought Stalin was blatantly spreading communism across the world. This was a threat to **democracy** and freedom. The mood of mistrust and suspicion deepened between the two sides. In January 1946, Stalin made a speech in which he said that **capitalism** was a threat to world peace. He could not see anything wrong in ensuring that the countries bordering the USSR were friendly and loyal to Moscow. President Truman was concerned about Stalin's attitude and said: "Unless Russia is faced with an iron fist and strong language, another war is in the making."

In March 1946, Truman invited Winston Churchill, the former British prime minister, to visit the United States. Churchill was worried about events in Eastern Europe, and voiced his concerns in public. He made a powerful speech at Westminster College in Fulton, Missouri, saying that Europe was now separated by an "iron curtain" that divided the democratic countries in the West from the communist East.

Churchill's Iron Curtain speech

*We understand that Russia needs to be secure on her Western frontiers from all renewal of German aggression. It is my duty, however, to place before you certain facts about the present position in Europe. From Stettin in the Baltic to Trieste in the Adriatic, an iron curtain has descended across the continent. The Communist Parties, which were very small in those eastern states of Europe, have been raised to pre-eminence and power and are seeking everywhere to obtain **totalitarian** control. This is certainly not the liberated Europe we fought to build up. Nor is it one which contains the essentials of permanent peace.*

Stalin reacted angrily to the speech, saying Churchill was stirring up trouble and that the USSR was merely defending itself from future invasions.

In 1947, Stalin tightened his control on Eastern Europe by introducing the Cominform (Communist Information Bureau). Its job was to coordinate the activities and policies of Communist Parties across Europe. Stalin made sure that all the party leaders were totally loyal and did as Moscow told them. However, Marshal Tito, president of communist Yugoslavia, refused to be ruled by the USSR. He argued with Stalin and this led to Yugoslavia being expelled from the Cominform in 1948.

Truman and Churchill drive through the streets of Fulton, Missouri on March 5, 1946. They are on their way to Westminster College, where Churchill was to make his famous Iron Curtain speech.

In March 1949, the Western powers formed the North Atlantic Treaty Organization (NATO) to defend themselves from attack. They said that if one member country of the alliance was attacked, the others would help it to fight back. In 1955, the USSR formed a similar alliance called the Warsaw Pact, which was made up of its Eastern European satellites.

MEMBERS OF NATO IN 1955	MEMBERS OF THE WARSAW PACT IN 1955
UNITED STATES	USSR
BELGIUM	ALBANIA
BRITAIN	BULGARIA
CANADA	CZECHOSLOVAKIA
DENMARK	EAST GERMANY
FRANCE	HUNGARY
GREECE	POLAND
ICELAND	ROMANIA
ITALY	
LUXEMBOURG	
NETHERLANDS	
NORWAY	
PORTUGAL	
SPAIN	
TURKEY	
WEST GERMANY	

The Truman Doctrine, 1947

In February 1947, President Truman was faced with a serious problem. In Greece, **communist guerrillas** were trying to take over the country. Britain had 40,000 troops in Greece helping the government fight the communists. Out of the blue, Ernest Bevin, the British foreign minister, told Truman that Britain could no longer afford to keep troops in Greece. Nearby, Turkey was also under threat. The **USSR** had placed troops on the Turkish border, waiting for the right moment to invade.

Truman's dramatic speech

Truman was worried. He feared that communism would spread across the world unless the United States took a stand. He wanted to prevent communism from spreading. On March 12, Truman made a dramatic speech to **Congress.** He said that the United States had to support free people from being taken over by "armed minorities" or "outside pressures." What he meant was that the United States had to stop communists from taking control of **democratic** countries, a policy that became known as the Truman Doctrine. Truman went on to say that communism was an evil system, in which there was no freedom of speech and living standards were low. Congress listened in silence. One member of Congress said that Truman had "scared the hell" out of them. Congress voted the sum of 400 million dollars to support Greece and Turkey. The money helped the Greek government to defeat the communists and keep the USSR out of Turkey.

President Truman makes his historic speech to Congress on March 12, 1947.

The Truman Doctrine

I believe it must be the policy of the United States to support all free peoples who are resisting attempted subjugation [control] by armed minorities or by outside pressures.

President Truman
March 12, 1947

Enter George C. Marshall

In January 1947, General George C. Marshall became the U.S. **secretary of state.** Marshall visited Western Europe in April 1947 and was shocked at the amount of damage caused by World War II. Towns, factories, farms, roads, and railways were still in urgent need of rebuilding, but there was no money to do it. Food was **rationed** and people were living miserable lives. Many countries in Western Europe had communist parties, and the Americans were concerned that people would vote them into power, believing that this would improve their lives.

In June 1947, Marshall made a speech at Harvard University in Massachusetts, in which he said that the United States would give money and equipment to help countries rebuild. This recovery program became known as the Marshall Plan. The offer was open to the USSR and the communist countries of Eastern Europe, but a suspicious Stalin ordered them not to take U.S. money. He said the real aim of the Marshall Plan was to make countries buy U.S. goods, thereby making it even more powerful.

Countries in Western Europe were enthusiastic about the Marshall Plan. Ernest Bevin said it was "like a lifeline to sinking men." By 1952, sixteen countries had received seventeen billion dollars to help them recover from the war. But both the Truman Doctrine and the Marshall Plan had driven a deeper wedge between the West and the East. The Cold War was now a fact of life.

A U.S. cartoon from the time shows the Marshall Plan providing Europe with a lifeline to recovery.

George Catlett Marshall (1880–1959)

Marshall served in the U.S. army in Europe during World War I. From 1939 to 1945 he was chief of staff of the U.S. army. He gained a reputation for being a good organizer.

When he became secretary of state in 1947, President Truman asked him if he could call him George. But Marshall was a believer in formality and he told the startled Truman: "No, General Marshall will do"! Marshall served as U.S. secretary of defense from 1950 to 1951 and was awarded the Nobel Peace prize in 1953.

The Berlin Airlift

At the end of World War II the United States, the **USSR,** Britain, and France divided Germany into four zones. Each country took control of one zone. Berlin, the capital city, was in the Soviet zone. It, too, was divided into four sectors, each under the control of one country. The four countries aimed to work together and, in time, sign a peace treaty with Germany. After this, all occupying troops would be pulled out. But things did not turn out as expected.

Germany had been completely ravaged by the war. Cities and factories lay in ruins. There was a great deal of poverty and food was scarce. The United States and Britain wanted to help their zones recover. Stalin, however, wanted compensation for the damage done to the USSR during the war. He tried to ensure that Germany would never again be strong enough to invade the USSR. The Soviets took factory machinery apart and transported it back to the USSR. They also set up a **communist** government in the Soviet zone.

The Berlin blockade and airlift from 1948 to 1949.

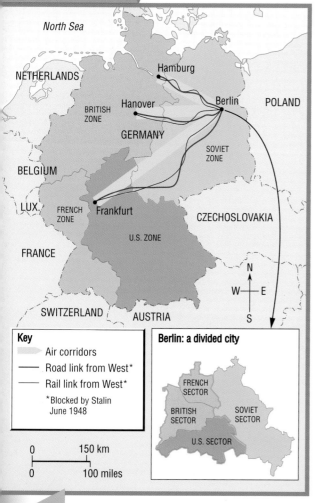

The United States, Britain, and France combined their zones of Germany and sectors of Berlin. Life here began to improve. There was food to buy and goods in the stores. In the Soviet zone, life remained hard. In June 1948, a new kind of money called the Deutschmark was introduced into the Western zones and Berlin. This would help to bring back prosperity to the German people. Stalin did not want anything to do with the new money. He was worried that people in East Berlin would want the same standard of living as people in the West. He decided to try to force the Western powers out of Berlin, so that all of it would be under Soviet control.

Berlin blockaded

Stalin's plan was to try to starve the people of West Berlin. On June 24, 1948, the Soviets closed all roads and railways running from the western half of Germany into Berlin. West Berlin relied on these routes for food and essential supplies, and Stalin hoped that the Western powers would do nothing and leave him in control of Berlin. He was to be disappointed. General Lucius Clay, the U.S. commander in Berlin, said: "If Berlin falls, Western Germany will be next. If we mean to hold Germany against communism, we must not budge."

It was decided to airlift supplies into West Berlin. From June 28, 1948 to May 11, 1949, **USAF, RAF,** and civilian planes made over 275,000 flights in and out of West Berlin, delivering over two million tons of supplies, including food, medicine, coal, clothing, and building supplies. It was a huge undertaking that cost the lives of 79 men. Eventually, Stalin realized that the Western powers were determined to keep West Berlin and he lifted the blockade. Supplies were once again allowed in over land.

Young children enthusiastically greet the arrival of a U.S. transport plane in Berlin in 1948.

The Western **Allies** realized that it was no longer possible to work with the USSR over the running of Germany. They took drastic action. On May 23, 1949, they merged the three Western zones to create the Federal Republic of Germany (West Germany), a **capitalist** and **democratic** country. In October 1949, the USSR reacted by making their Eastern zone the German Democratic Republic (East Germany), a communist country under the influence of Moscow. Germany was to remain a divided country for the next 41 years.

The candy bomber

Lieutenant Gail Halvorsen was a U.S. pilot who took part in the Berlin airlift. He felt sorry for the children of Berlin and wanted to cheer them up. He started "Operation Little Vittles" ("vittles" means food). Halvorsen obtained as many packets of candy and chewing gum as he could, and tied them to small "parachutes" made of handkerchiefs. He and his crew then air-dropped the candy over Berlin. News of the operation spread and soon U.S. candy manufacturers were sending candy to Europe for Halvorsen to drop. By January 1949, he had dropped over 250,000 "parachutes" of candy for the delighted children, who were not used to such treats in postwar Berlin.

Superpower Rivalry, 1945–1969

The arms race

When the United States dropped the first atomic bomb on the Japanese city of Hiroshima on August 6, 1945, it heralded the start of what became known as the arms race. Hiroshima was flattened and 80,000 people were killed instantly. Thousands more died later from **radiation sickness** and burns. The world was shocked by the power of the bomb.

After 1945, as the Cold War started, relations between the West and East worsened. The **USSR** felt insecure, as it did not have the atomic bomb, so Stalin ordered his scientists to produce one quickly. By 1949 they had succeeded. Now it was the turn of the United States and its **allies** to worry; an arms race was under way.

On November 1, 1952, the U.S. exploded the first hydrogen bomb on the Pacific island of Eniwetok. It was a hundred times more powerful than the atomic bomb. On August 14, 1953, the Soviets announced that they, too, had successfully tested a hydrogen bomb. The U.S. president, Dwight Eisenhower, decided that the United States needed to build up a massive stockpile of nuclear weapons. This made economic sense, as they were actually cheaper than **conventional weapons.** One U.S. politician said that nuclear weapons gave "more bang for the buck"!

In 1957, the USSR built the first Intercontinental Ballistic Missile (ICBM). These rockets were able to carry nuclear warheads and could be launched at targets thousands of miles (kilometers) away. The United States soon caught up and by 1958 had its own ICBMs. Missile sites were built in NATO countries close to the USSR, such as Turkey, and pointed at Soviet cities. When the USSR tried to place missiles in Cuba in 1962, it brought the world to the brink of a **nuclear war.** Both sides now had enough weapons to destroy the earth several times over. They had spent vast sums on nuclear weapons that they hoped they would never use. The idea was to deter the other side. If one side attacked, the other would retaliate and the result would be mutually assured destruction (or MAD for short).

The course of an ICBM missile. It would take about 30 minutes for a missile to reach the United States from the USSR. Short-range U.S. missiles based in Turkey would hit the USSR in a matter of minutes.

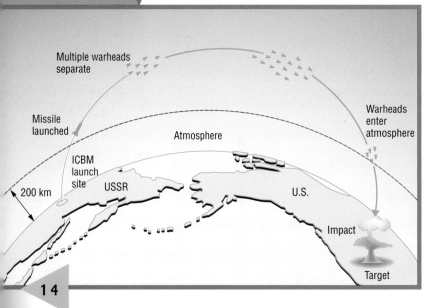

Multiple warheads separate

Missile launched

Atmosphere

Warheads enter atmosphere

ICBM launch site

USSR

U.S.

200 km

Impact

Target

The space race

In 1957 the Soviets launched the world's first satellite into space, and in April 1961 Yuri Gagarin became the first human into space. In a flight lasting 108 minutes, he orbited the earth in a *Vostok* spaceship and returned safely. It was an amazing **propaganda** success for the Soviets, for they claimed that their scientists were in front of those in the West. On February 20, 1962, John H. Glenn became the first American to orbit the earth. In 1963, the Soviets had another success when Valentina Tereshkova became the first woman in space. Which side would be the first to land men on the moon? The Americans won the race when Neil Armstrong and Edwin "Buzz" Aldrin walked on the moon on July 21, 1969.

Edwin "Buzz" Aldrin walks on the moon with the lunar module in the background. Neil Armstrong can be seen reflected in Aldrin's visor.

Nuclear paranoia and protest

During the Cold War, people lived in fear of a nuclear war. Americans built nuclear fallout shelters in their gardens. U.S. schoolchildren were taught fallout drills called "duck and cover." It was said that one hundred Soviet missiles hitting a small island such as Britain would kill 40 million people. In the late 1950s large protest movements evolved, such as the Campaign for Nuclear Disarmament (CND) in Britain, whose members included many eminent scientists, writers, and politicians. Every Easter, CND held a large march from the Atomic Weapons Research Establishment at Aldermaston to London. They called for the government to "ban the bomb." One marcher said: "We're marching because it is all we can do to express our hostility towards a policy that is bound to lead to nuclear catastrophe and widespread destruction." The British government, however, took little notice.

Cold War Spy Scandals

During the Cold War, the level of mistrust was so high that both sides spied on each other to try to gather military secrets and other information. In 1947, President Truman set up the Central **Intelligence** Agency (CIA) whose job was to "collect and coordinate foreign intelligence." Shortly after the death of Stalin in 1953, the **USSR** set up the **KGB** (Committee for State Security) to spy on the West.

Both the CIA and the KGB recruited spies. At the height of the Cold War, each side had up to 4,000 secret agents working for them. One of the earliest spies was Klaus Fuchs, a German-born British scientist. Fuchs was a member of the team that developed the atomic bomb for the United States. In 1950, he was arrested in London for spying for the USSR. He had passed detailed drawings of the bomb to the USSR. This helped the Soviets to build their own atomic bomb much more quickly. Fuchs was imprisoned for fourteen years, but was released in 1959.

A spy in the sky: the U-2 incident, 1960

In early 1960 there was a thaw in the Cold War, when relationships between the two sides began to improve. A summit meeting in Paris was planned for May 14, when it was hoped there would be friendly talks.

On May 1 a U.S. U-2 spy plane, piloted by Francis Gary Powers, was shot down over the USSR. The Soviets found cameras on board the plane and said that Powers had been on a spying mission. They developed the film and found hundreds of photographs of Soviet military bases. President Eisenhower of the United States said that the plane must have gone off course and the cameras had been observing cloud patterns. Khrushchev, the Soviet leader, was furious.

The wreck of the U-2 spy plane piloted by Francis Gary Powers.

When the two leaders met in Paris, Khrushchev demanded a public apology from the United States. Eisenhower refused and the Soviet leader stormed out of the meeting. A planned visit to Moscow by Eisenhower was called off. The thaw was over.

Gary Powers was put on trial in the USSR and sentenced to ten years in prison. He served seventeen months of his sentence before being exchanged with a Soviet spy who was in prison in the United States.

Oleg Penkovsky, a Soviet colonel, spied for the West during 1962–63, providing the United States with details of the USSR's plans during the Cuban Missile Crisis. In 1963, the KGB arrested Penkovsky in Moscow after he was seen with Greville Wynne, his British contact. The USSR claimed that Penkovsky had passed over 500 top-secret military documents to the West. He was executed by firing squad. Wynne was sentenced to eight years in prison.

In 1963, Britain was rocked by the "Profumo Affair." John Profumo was the War Minister in Harold Macmillan's Conservative government. An acquaintance of Profumo was friends with a man named Eugene Ivanov, a diplomat at the Soviet Embassy in London. The British government feared that Profumo had given his acquaintance secret information, which she then passed on to Ivanov. Profumo denied this, but he was forced to resign.

Melita Norwood as seen in September 1999. She said she "gave bomb secrets to the USSR so it could stand up to the West."

Recent scandals

In 1994, Aldrich Ames, a CIA officer, admitted that he had spied for the KGB during the Cold War. He told a court in Virginia, that he had been paid a total of 2.7 million dollars by the KGB for handing over secret information. More seriously, he told the Soviets the names of 25 agents working for the CIA in Moscow. Ten of them were rooted out and shot by the KGB. Ames was sentenced to life imprisonment.

In September 1999, the British public was shocked by the news that an 87-year-old grandmother, Melita Norwood, had spied for the USSR during the Cold War. When she had worked as the personal secretary to the director of the British Non-Ferrous Metals Research Association, Norwood had access to secret documents about Britain's atomic bomb. Code-named "Hola," she passed this information on to the KGB. The British government, however, decided not to prosecute her.

The Korean War, 1950–1953

The main phases of fighting in the Korean War from 1950 to 1953.

Between 1910 and 1945, Korea was controlled by Japan. In 1945, Soviet troops entered Korea north of the 38th parallel of latitude and U.S. troops went into the south. The Japanese were forced to surrender. Like Germany, Korea became a divided country. The Soviets set up a **communist** government in North Korea under the leadership of Kim Il Sung, and in South Korea, an anti-communist government was established under Dr. Syngman Rhee. Both men claimed to be the rightful leader of the whole of Korea. In 1948, Soviet and U.S. troops left and the problem of who should rule Korea was handed over to the **United Nations (UN).**

War!

On June 25, 1950, North Korean troops invaded South Korea. The Americans were worried that South Korea would be taken over by the North. The United Nations decided to send a force to help the South Koreans. At the time, the Soviets were absent from the United Nations. If they had been there they would have voted against the decision and the UN would not have been able to do anything.

The North Korean army was well-organized and equipped with Soviet-made weapons. It virtually overran South Korea and was closing in on Pusan. On September 15, 1950, UN forces commanded by U.S. General Douglas MacArthur and made up of soldiers from sixteen countries, including the United States, Australia, and Britain, landed at Inchon. By the end of September, the North Koreans had been pushed back over the 38th parallel. MacArthur then drove them northward toward the Yalu River and the Chinese border. China was a communist country and it did not want a U.S.-led UN force so close to its border. So, on October 16, 250,000 Chinese troops were sent to help the North Koreans. The UN forces were pushed back to just south of the 38th parallel.

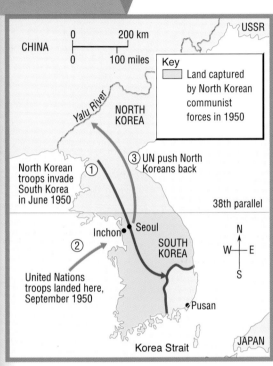

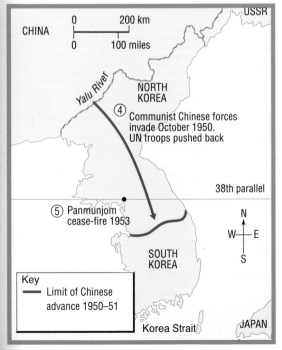

MacArthur dismissed

Truman now wanted an end to the war. The UN forces had expelled the North Koreans from the South and saved it from communism. Truman was satisfied with this. MacArthur, however, wanted to go on with the war. He wanted air strikes against targets in China and said he would consider using the nuclear bomb. Truman knew this was an outrageous idea, as bombing China could bring the **USSR** into the conflict and start World War III. MacArthur still disagreed, so Truman dismissed him. In his farewell speech to **Congress** on April 19, 1951, MacArthur said: "You cannot appease or otherwise surrender to communism in Asia without undermining our efforts to halt its advance in Europe." His words reflected the extreme feelings about communism at the time. Limited fighting went on in Korea for another two years, until in 1953 a cease-fire was agreed at Panmunjom and the war came to end.

U.S. marines launch an artillery attack on the enemy in Korea in 1951.

The results of the Korean War

Korea was still a divided country, but communism had been stopped from spreading into South Korea. The war brought heavy casualties with the United States losing over 50,000 men. Losses of other UN soldiers totaled about 3,200. An estimated one million civilians lost their lives. There was also widespread damage to roads, railways, factories, and towns. Relations between the United States and the USSR were now very strained.

Women in the Korean War

Over 120,000 U.S. women were on service in Korea. Most of them were in the Army Nurse Corps working in Mobile Army Surgical Hospitals. Some served as flight nurses: they flew into war zones to evacuate the injured, tending wounds on the flight back to base. Perhaps the most famous flight nurse was Lillian Kinkela Keil. She flew on over 200 evacuation missions in World War II and came out of retirement to fly on missions in Korea.

Revolution in Hungary, 1956

When Josef Stalin died in 1953, he was replaced by Nikita Khrushchev as the leader of the **USSR.** Stalin had ruled the USSR's **satellite** countries in Eastern Europe with an iron fist. Everyone had to do as Stalin told them or suffer the consequences. Khrushchev, however, seemed to have a more relaxed approach, and talked of existing peacefully side by side with the West.

In February 1956, Khrushchev made a speech in which he said that Stalin had been a brutal tyrant who had used fear and terror to stay in power. People in the countries of Eastern Europe were encouraged by this speech. They thought that Khrushchev would give them more freedom in running their countries and there would be less interference from the USSR.

Riots in Poland

In June 1956, factory workers in Poland rioted when the government raised food prices. The Polish army could not control the rioters, so the USSR sent in tanks to restore order. Khrushchev flew to Poland for talks. He agreed that the popular Vladislav Gomulka should become the Polish leader. The trouble in Poland faded away. But there were more problems waiting for the USSR.

A wrecked statue of Stalin in a Budapest street, 1956. This illustrates the Hungarians' anger at Soviet control of their country.

Fighting in Budapest

Hungary had been a Soviet satellite since 1946. The Soviets put a **communist** government into power that answered to the orders of Moscow. Many Hungarians were angry because there was a shortage of food and they were not allowed to criticize the government. People did not like being controlled by the USSR and wanted Soviet troops to get out of Hungary.

On October 23, 1956, over 300,000 people took to the streets of Budapest, the capital city. They tore down statues of Stalin and demanded greater freedom. The police opened fire as the crowd chanted, "Go home Russians." To please the Hungarians and restore order, Khrushchev allowed the popular Imre Nagy to become the prime minister.

Nagy began to change Hungary. He said that free elections would be held and Hungary would leave the Warsaw Pact. This was too much for Khrushchev. If he allowed Hungary more freedom, then all the other satellite countries would demand the same. He decided to act.

On November 4, 1956, over 6,000 Soviet tanks invaded Hungary to bring the country "back into line." There was heavy street fighting and an estimated 30,000 Hungarians were killed. Budapest suffered heavy damage, with 8,000 houses being destroyed. About 200,000 people fled the country for good. Nagy was arrested and hanged in Moscow in 1958. Khrushchev's message was clear: the USSR would not put up with any of its satellite countries trying to break free of Soviet control.

A Hungarian family, who have fled their home, arrive in Klingenbach in Austria, November 1956.

Escape from Hungary

In 1956, Veronica Varga was a 4-year-old child growing up in Budapest. Her parents decided to flee Hungary, as they were both wanted for "questioning" by the Soviets. On November 28, they boarded a train to take them on the long journey to the Austrian border. The train was virtually empty. The guard told them the train would be searched by Soviet troops when it reached the border. He said they had a better chance of getting across the border if they continued on foot. The train stopped in the countryside and eight passengers, including Veronica and her parents, got off the train. They were met by a group of local farmers and hidden in a barn. The next evening, guided by the farmers, the group set off for the border. Along the way, other people joined them, so that soon the group numbered 50 people. They had to wade through swamps and find their way through thick forests. After about four hours they reached the border, which was protected by a barbed-wire fence, watch-towers, and armed guards. They cut a hole through the fence and crawled through into Austria. People cried tears of joy and sorrow. They were safe, but might never see their homeland, family, and friends again. Veronica and her parents eventually settled in California.

The Berlin Wall Goes Up

After Stalin lifted the blockade in 1949, Berlin remained a divided city. During the 1950s, West Berlin received large amounts of money under the Marshall Plan. This part of the city was rebuilt and soon began to prosper. There was plenty of food in the stores, and there were cinemas, theaters, cafés, and nightclubs. West Berliners could enjoy life again. Above all, they were able to vote in free elections and speak their minds without fear of arrest.

In 1961, the Berlin Wall was built to isolate West Berlin from Soviet territory. The "Country Wall" separated West Berlin from East Germany.

East Berlin, under **communist** rule, was a harsh place. Many buildings remained abandoned and there was very little to buy in the stores. Most people lived in dull apartment blocks and few owned cars, refrigerators, or washing machines, which were becoming common in Western Europe and the United States. East Berliners did not enjoy freedom of speech and lived in fear of being arrested by the secret police. But, despite these differences, people could still travel wherever they liked in the city. Underground trains and trams ran between the East and West. East Berliners were free to visit friends in the West, and over 50,000 of them traveled to work there each day.

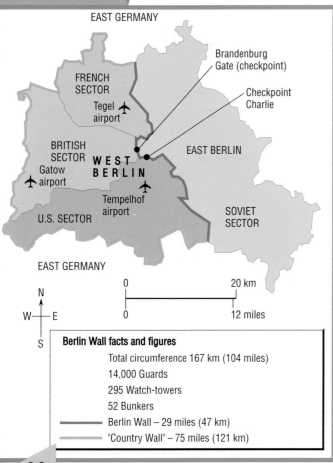

EAST GERMANY

FRENCH SECTOR

Tegel airport

Brandenburg Gate (checkpoint)

Checkpoint Charlie

BRITISH SECTOR
Gatow airport

W E S T B E R L I N

EAST BERLIN

Tempelhof airport

U.S. SECTOR

SOVIET SECTOR

EAST GERMANY

```
        0              20 km
  N     |---------------|
W-+-E   0              12 miles
  S
```

Berlin Wall facts and figures

Total circumference 167 km (104 miles)
14,000 Guards
295 Watch-towers
52 Bunkers
—— Berlin Wall – 29 miles (47 km)
—— "Country Wall" – 75 miles (121 km)

Many East Germans wanted a better standard of living and **defected** to the West. They crossed into West Berlin, where they settled or they caught a plane to West Germany. Most of the defectors were under the age of 45 and many had useful skills. Defectors included teachers, lawyers, doctors, and engineers. There were more job opportunities in the West and wages were higher.

The difference between East and West Berlin showed in clothes. When we went across we always had bags full of things. Like every other family from the West we took fresh fruit which was unobtainable in the East, nicer clothes, and soap. You were always loaded when you went across. In those days there was no Wall, so you didn't have your bags checked. You could cross anywhere where the street went across the border.

Margit Hosseini, a resident of West Berlin, describes life before the Wall went up.

Kennedy and Khrushchev

Soon, more than 200,000 people a year were defecting to the West, and East Germany was losing most of its skilled workers. In June 1961, Nikita Khrushchev, the Soviet leader, met the new president of the United States, John F. Kennedy, in Vienna. Khrushchev thought Kennedy was inexperienced and would crack under pressure. He told Kennedy that he wanted the Western powers out of Berlin by the end of the year or there would be war. Kennedy took him at his word and told the U.S. army to prepare. He also advised Americans to build nuclear shelters.

The Wall

Two months later Khrushchev backed down. He realized that Kennedy was determined to hang on to West Berlin, but somehow he had to put a stop to the flood of people defecting.

Khrushchev and the East German leader, Walter Ulbricht, decided to build a wall that would seal East Berlin off from the West. In the early hours of August 13, 1961, East German workmen started to erect a barbed-wire fence between East and West Berlin. As word spread, people went into the streets to jeer at the workmen, who were protected by armed guards. Near the Brandenburg Gate, in the center of Berlin, a crowd pulled down the barbed wire. Guards turned on water hoses and fired tear gas at the crowd. The East Germans stopped underground trains and trams going into the West. East German workers going to work in the West were turned back by border guards. For a time there was chaos. The Western powers did nothing to stop the Wall being built. Kennedy said, "a wall is better than a war."

Behind the Berlin Wall is the famous Brandenburg Gate, which was built in 1791 as a tollgate for the collection of taxes from people entering the city. The board says: "Attention, you are now leaving West Berlin."

Kennedy visits Berlin

On June 26, 1963, John F. Kennedy visited Berlin. Over one million West Berliners turned out to hear him speak. He gave an inspired speech in which he said the now famous words: "Ich bin ein Berliner." He had meant to say "I am a Berliner," but this actually translates as "I am a doughnut.". . . Nevertheless, the crowd cheered and clapped their approval.

Escaping to the West

When the Berlin Wall was built, it divided friends and families. Before the Wall, people who lived in the West had been able to visit their relations and friends in the East. Now they were permanently separated. Until 1963, they were not even allowed to exchange letters.

Early escapes

In the first days of the Wall there were numerous escapes from the East to West. A Volkswagen car was driven at high speed through the barbed wire, and some people escaped by swimming across the Teltow Canal. In one street, Bernauerstrasse, blocks of apartments backed on to the Wall and some of the residents jumped out of high windows into blankets held by waiting West Berliners. It was not long before East German guards bricked up the windows. Later the apartments were torn down. On August 24, 1961, Gunter Litfin became the first person to be shot dead while trying to escape. Another 40 people were to suffer the same fate over the next twelve months.

East German border guards carry the dead body of Peter Fechter away.

Murderers! Murderers!

On August 17, 1962, seventeen-year-old Peter Fechter and his friend, Helmut Kulbeik, tried to escape over the Wall to the West near the crossing-point, Checkpoint Charlie. The Wall here was built out of cinder blocks and capped with rolls of barbed wire. It was about six and a half feet (two meters) high. They hid in an abandoned house before picking their moment, when they sprinted to the Wall and began to climb it. Unfortunately, they were spotted by the guards, who opened fire with their machine guns. Helmut managed to scramble over the top to safety, but Peter was hit in the back. He slumped to the ground, bleeding heavily. People in West Berlin heard the shooting and stood on car roofs to look over the Wall. They were furious at what they saw and chanted, "Murderers! Murderers!" at the East Germans. Apart from throwing some bandages to him, not one guard tried to help Peter. He lay motionless, screaming for help and in obvious pain. Within an hour, he had bled to death. His body was thrown into a van, which was then driven away by the guards. The whole event was recorded by cameras and shown on television in the West. People were shocked at the brutality of the killing. In West Berlin, there were protest marches and calls for the Americans to bulldoze the Wall down. The calls were ignored and the Wall stayed in place for another 27 years.

Strengthening the Wall

During the 1960s, the East Germans reinforced the Wall, which made it more difficult to escape. The cinder blocks were replaced by solid concrete, for example. Behind the Wall on the Eastern side there was a piece of open ground about 328 feet (100 m) wide, which was known as "death strip." This was overlooked by tall watchtowers and floodlights. Guards with dogs patrolled constantly. It was an awesome barrier. Even so, it did not stop East Germans from trying to escape.

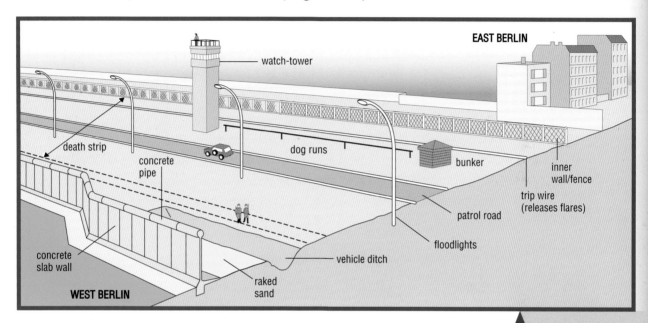

Later attempts at escape

People used many ingenious ways to escape. Some hid in cable drums that were due to be taken to the West. For awhile, people hid in secret compartments in specially built cars, but the guards grew wise to this, so every car entering the West from the East was thoroughly checked. One man hid his girlfriend and mother in his sports car and drove it at high speed under the barrier. The guards were so shocked, they did nothing. Specialist escape organizations were formed: a group led by Wolfgang Fuchs dug seven tunnels under the Wall through which about 500 people were guided to freedom. The longest tunnel was 394 feet (120 m) long and even had lighting and ventilation. Another escape organizer, Wolf Quasner, specialized in forging diplomatic passports and visas. These were smuggled into East Berlin and sold to people who wished to escape to the West.

As the years wore on, fewer attempts were made to escape. Life in East Berlin improved a little as wages rose and people could afford to buy a few home comforts, such as televisions and washing machines.

The Berlin Wall was heavily fortified, making it almost impossible to cross.

The Cuban Missile Crisis, 1962

Since 1898, U.S. firms had controlled most of Cuba's economy. The United States also had a large naval base at Guantánamo in southeast Cuba. In 1959 Fidel Castro overthrew Fulgencio Batista, the corrupt Cuban leader. The new government immediately took control of all industry and businesses, most of which had been owned by Americans. This angered the Americans and in 1961 they supported an invasion of Cuba, the aim of which was to remove Castro from power. About 1,500 exiled Cubans landed at the Bay of Pigs, but were easily beaten by Castro's troops. Castro's dislike of the United States deepened and he made friends with Khrushchev, who was happy to send him money and arms. Castro then announced that Cuba was to be a **communist** country.

Crisis

On October 14, 1962, Major Richard Heyser's U–2 spy plane flew over Cuba and photographed Soviet nuclear missile sites being built. The threat to the United States was obvious, as Cuba is just 93 miles (150 km) away from Florida's coast. From there, Soviet missiles could be fired at most U.S. cities.

Soviet missile sites on Cuba as photographed by a U-2 plane. The photograph was taken from 34 miles (4,500 m) up in the air, but was so accurate that it was possible to read the writing on the side of the missiles!

MISSILE ERECTOR
CABLE
MISSILE SHELTER TENT
TRACKED PRIME MOVERS
OXIDIZER TANK TRAILERS
FUEL TANK TRAILERS

An alarmed President Kennedy called together a committee of twelve advisers to discuss what action should be taken. Kennedy secretly recorded the conversation, and the tape shows the drama of the occasion. The committee had three stark choices:

1. Bomb the missile bases and other targets in Cuba.
2. Invade Cuba.
3. Put a naval blockade around Cuba to stop Soviet ships from delivering missiles.

The **USAF** told Kennedy that an air strike could cost up to 20,000 lives. After a drawn-out argument it was decided to blockade Cuba. Any ships heading for Cuba with cargoes of "offensive weapons" would be turned back. Some members of the committee thought that Kennedy was being soft. For example, General LeMay told him: "I just don't see any other solution except direct military action right now. A blockade would be considered by a lot of our friends to be a pretty weak response."

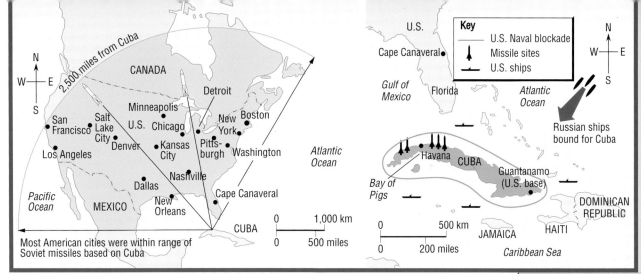

Most American cities were within range of Soviet missiles based on Cuba

On October 24, U.S. warships blockaded Cuba to wait for the Soviet ships they knew were on their way. Would the Soviets try to break the blockade or would they turn back? The world held its breath. Thankfully they stopped and turned back. But there was still the question of what to do about the missiles already sited on Cuba.

On October 26, Khrushchev, the Soviet leader, wrote to Kennedy saying he was willing to remove the missiles if Kennedy guaranteed that the United States would not invade Cuba. Before Kennedy had a chance to answer, on October 27 a second letter arrived from Khrushchev. This one demanded that the United States remove the missiles it had placed in Turkey. Kennedy was puzzled. How should he reply? His brother Robert, the U.S. **attorney general,** advised him to ignore the second letter and just reply to the first. President Kennedy took the advice and told Khrushchev that he would not invade Cuba. On October 28, Khrushchev announced on Radio Moscow that he would remove the missiles from Cuba. Castro was furious that Khrushchev withdrew the Soviet missiles from Cuba without asking him first, but the crisis was over.

If Khrushchev had not backed down, the world could have been plunged into a **nuclear war,** but many people in the **USSR** thought their country had lost face. People in the West were grateful that Khrushchev had not pushed the United States any further and that a potential World War III had been avoided.

As a result of the crisis, a direct telephone "hot line" was put in between the Kremlin in Moscow and the White House. This would enable the leaders of the United States and USSR to talk directly to each other, rather than having to correspond by letter. In 1963, both sides signed the Test Ban Treaty, which was supposed to stop the testing of nuclear bombs in the atmosphere, underwater, and in space.

The Cuban Missile Crisis, 1962. The Soviet missiles had a range of 2,600 miles (4,183 km). The map shows how far across the United States this would reach and how the United States blockaded Cuba.

Monday October 29, 1962

NEW YORK MIRROR

K BOWS!
Will Pull Out Missiles
Kennedy Made No Deals

How the New York Mirror reported the end of the Cuban Missile Crisis. "K" was the U.S. nickname for Krushchev.

The Prague Spring, 1968

Czechoslovakia had **communism** imposed upon it in 1948. From that moment, no other political parties were allowed and the country came under the influence of the **USSR.** Following the example of the Soviets, Czech industry concentrated on producing steel and coal. Very few household goods such as furniture, cameras, radios, and fashionable clothes were produced, so the Czech people had a low standard of living. Wages were lower than in the West and for many people life was drab. Under the communists, if anyone criticized the government they would be thrown into prison. Newspapers and the movies were **censored** and there were no free elections.

In 1967, there was a slump in trade. Factories were forced to cut down on production, and wages were lowered. Antonin Novotny, the hard-line Czech leader, did nothing to improve the situation. In January 1968, Novotny was dismissed by the Communist Party and replaced as leader by Alexander Dubček.

The people of Prague try to persuade Soviet tank crews to go home, August 1968.

Reforms

Dubček wanted Czechoslovakia to stay a communist country loyal to Moscow, but he believed that people should have more freedom and a higher standard of living. He called it communism "with a human face." In March 1968 Dubček announced a number of reforms. Newspapers would no longer be censored and people would be free to criticize the government if they wished. Dubček also promised that political parties other than the Communist Party would be allowed. Czech people would be able to travel abroad more, and people who had been imprisoned for criticizing the government were released. These reforms became known as the Prague Spring.

Invasion

The Soviet leader, Leonid Brezhnev, was worried by events in Czechoslovakia. Recalling the events in Hungary in 1956, he feared that if the Czech people were given more freedom the other **satellite** countries would want the same. Brezhnev did not trust Dubček and believed Dubček would take Czechoslovakia out of the Warsaw Pact. The time had come for action. On August 21, 1968, over 500,000 Soviet troops supported by smaller units from Poland, Hungary, East Germany, and Bulgaria invaded Czechoslovakia. Crowds of people went into the streets of the capital city, Prague, to confront the Soviet tanks. The famous Czech Olympic athlete, Emil Zatopek, made an emotional speech, saying that the Russians should go home. Some tanks were set on fire but, in general, the protesters stayed calm. Some people climbed onto the tanks to ask the soldiers to go home.

Dubček, however, was arrested and taken to Moscow. He was made to give up his program of reforms and had to agree to Soviet troops staying in Czechoslovakia. In 1969, Gustav Husak, a hard-line communist, replaced Dubček as leader. The Soviets knew that Husak would do as Moscow told him.

By invading Czechoslovakia, Brezhnev made it clear that he was going to keep Eastern Europe firmly under Soviet control. He issued the Brezhnev Doctrine, which said that if one satellite country tried to move towards **democracy,** it was the duty of other communist countries to stop it.

A large crowd turned out to pay their last respects to Jan Palach, January 1969.

Jan Palach

On January 19, 1969, Jan Palach, a 21-year-old Czech student, set fire to himself in Wenceslas Square in Prague. He was protesting against the Soviet invasion and the fact that Dubček's reforms had been abolished. Palak died from his injuries on January 21. A huge crowd of 800,000 turned out to watch his funeral in Prague. They shouted, "Russians go home." It was an emotional occasion and gave people the chance to vent their hatred of the USSR.

Two months later there were great celebrations when the Czech ice-hockey team beat the USSR 4–3 in the World Ice Hockey Championships in Stockholm, Sweden. An audience of six million Czech people watched the match on television. They looked upon the victory as revenge against the Soviet invaders.

War in Vietnam

During the late nineteenth century, French troops conquered Vietnam, in Southeast Asia, and it remained a French colony until the outbreak of World War II. In 1940, the Japanese forced the French out of Vietnam, but they returned in 1946. A **communist** group called the **Vietminh,** led by Ho Chi Minh, drove them out for good in 1954.

At a conference in Geneva, Vietnam was split into two separate countries: North Vietnam with a communist government headed by Ho Chi Minh, and South Vietnam with an anti-communist government. The conference intended free elections to be held in 1956, and that the winner would rule a united Vietnam, but the elections were never held.

The government in South Vietnam soon became very unpopular. It was made up of greedy landowners who did nothing to help the peasant farmers. The government came under attack from **Vietcong guerrilla** soldiers supported by the communist North. The Americans believed that North Vietnam wanted to take over the South and turn the whole of Vietnam into a communist country. They felt that if Vietnam fell to communism, other countries in Southeast Asia would follow, rather like a row of upright dominoes being toppled.

A map of Southeast Asia during the Vietnam War.

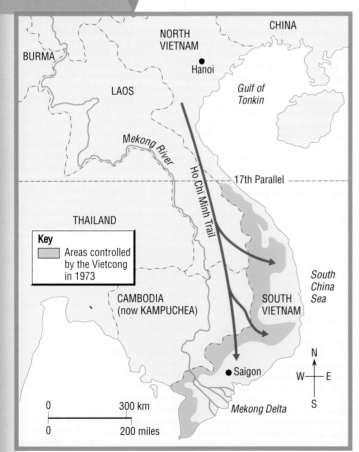

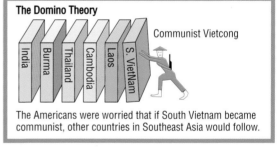

The Domino Theory

Communist Vietcong

India · Burma · Thailand · Cambodia · Laos · S. Vietnam

The Americans were worried that if South Vietnam became communist, other countries in Southeast Asia would follow.

So, the United States sent money and advisers to help the government of South Vietnam fight the Vietcong. Gradually, the Vietcong won the support of many South Vietnamese peasants, and by 1961 they controlled over half of South Vietnam. North Vietnam supplied the Vietcong with weapons which were carried down a jungle track called the Ho Chi Minh Trail. In 1962, President Kennedy sent U.S. troops to help the South Vietnamese. When Kennedy was assassinated in 1963, Lyndon Johnson became president of the United States.

Johnson steps up the war

In 1964, North Vietnamese gunboats fired on a U.S. warship, *USS Maddox* in the Gulf of Tonkin. **Congress** gave Johnson permission to step up the war. In 1965, B-52 bombers began "Operation Rolling Thunder," a series of bombing raids on the North. Over a three-year period more bombs were dropped on Vietnam than by all the sides in World War II. By 1968, there were over 500,000 U.S. troops in Vietnam. The Vietcong, however, were difficult to fight. They hid in the jungle and carried out surprise attacks. They did not wear a uniform so it was impossible to tell them apart from ordinary peasants. On January 30, 1968, the Vietcong launched the Tet Offensive, a major attack on Saigon and other South Vietnamese cities. The attack took the U.S. troops by surprise. Although the Vietcong were eventually driven back, many Americans came to believe that the war should be brought to an end.

A U.S. B-52 bomber in action during the Vietnam War. These bombers flew at a height of nine miles (15,000 meters) up in the air and carried 28 bombs, each weighing more than two tons.

In 1969 Richard Nixon, the new U.S. president, promised to scale down the United States' involvement in the war. He began to withdraw troops and provided South Vietnam with weapons to defend itself. Nixon said he would seek "peace with honor." In 1973, the Paris Peace Agreement was signed which ended the United States' participation in Vietnam. By 1975, North Vietnamese troops had overrun the South. Vietnam became a united country under a communist government.

WAR FACTS

U.S. SOLDIERS KILLED	58,132
AUSTRALIAN SOLDIERS KILLED	501
NORTH VIETNAMESE AND VIETCONG SOLDIERS KILLED	900,000
SOUTH VIETNAMESE SOLDIERS KILLED	200,000
CIVILIANS KILLED	500,000
COST TO U.S. TAXPAYERS	$150 BILLION
COST TO AUSTRALIAN TAXPAYERS	$218.4 MILLION

LARGE AREAS OF VIETNAMESE FOREST AND FARMLAND WERE DESTROYED OR POISONED BY CHEMICALS.

Americans Protest

When the U.S. government first got involved in Vietnam it had the support of the majority of the population. Those who opposed the war were **pacifists** or members of religious groups. In November 1965, Norman Morrison, a strict **Quaker,** set fire to himself near the Pentagon building in Washington, D.C. He died from his burns. Morrison had read a report about innocent Vietnamese villagers being burned by napalm dropped by U.S. planes. He felt so bad about this that he was driven to take his own life in protest. The nation was shocked by Morrison's death. Opposition to the war had started to gain momentum.

Anti-Vietnam War protesters march down Pennsylvania Avenue toward a rally at the Washington Monument in 1969.

In April 1965, a group called Students for a Democratic Society organized a protest in Washington, D.C. attended by 20,000 people. A "teach-in" was held at the University of Michigan, where people discussed the war and whether the United States should be involved in it. Superstar singers such as Joan Baez and Bob Dylan wrote songs protesting against the war.

The war escalated as the 1960s wore on and more and more Americans were drafted (enlisted) into the army to serve in Vietnam. Most of them were from the working class rather than the middle class. Twenty percent of the draftees were African-American, yet they only made up ten percent of the U.S. population.

The horrors of war brought home

The war was widely reported. Every day people watched the news on television. They began to question why the United States had got itself into such a terrible war. Thousands of young Americans were being killed: in one week in May 1968, 5,550 U.S. soldiers were killed.

The protests in the United States became more defiant and militant. Men drafted to fight refused to go to Vietnam. Many burned their draft papers in public. Others fled the country and went to Canada to avoid being sent to Vietnam. The world heavyweight boxing champion,

Muhammad Ali, refused to serve in the army and was stripped of his world title, but his action inspired others to resist the draft. Demonstrations often turned violent as protesters clashed with the police. In 1969, the U.S. public was shocked to learn about the killing of over 300 civilians by U.S. troops in My Lai, a village in South Vietnam. This fueled opposition to the war. One political commentator said: "How can we Americans support actions like this?"

The protests continued, with students strongly voicing their anti-war feelings. On May 1, 1970, Nixon said that student protesters were "bums" who should get on with their studying. Three days later, tragic events took place at Kent State University.

Tragedy at Kent State University, Ohio

On April 30, 1970, there was anger in the United States when Nixon secretly ordered U.S. troops to invade Cambodia. On May 4, students at Kent State University, near Cleveland, Ohio, held an anti-war demonstration. National Guardsmen fired their guns into the crowd, killing four students. Two of them were on their way to class and were not even part of the demonstration. Anger and fury spread across the United States. There were strikes at almost 500 universities and the rock band, Crosby, Stills, Nash & Young recorded a song called "Ohio." A commission was set up to investigate the killings. In its report it said: "A nation driven to use the weapons of war upon its youth is a nation on the edge of chaos."

A horrified student holds her head in anguish as she looks at one of the dead students lying in a pool of blood.

By now soldiers were deserting the army, while others sewed peace badges onto their uniforms. In the United States, the GIs Against the War Movement was formed. They argued that the war was a fiasco and immoral. They said: "We are forced to fight in a war we did not create and in which we don't believe." In 1973, the Americans withdrew their last troops from Vietnam. The protest movement had played its part in the United States' decision to end the war.

Détente, 1968–1979

Between about 1968 and 1979 there was a period of **détente** between the United States and the **USSR.** During this time, both sides tried to be more friendly toward each other and there was less tension. There were several reasons for this. By 1968, they each had about the same number of nuclear weapons and they knew that a major war would destroy the planet. President Nixon felt it was time to be friendlier toward the USSR to try to reduce the threat of **nuclear war.** The USSR, under Leonid Brezhnev, also wanted friendlier relations. The money spent on nuclear weapons would be better spent on improving living conditions in the USSR.

Then there was the issue of China, the world's biggest **communist** country. In 1960 the USSR and China fell out. This suited the West, as the spread of communism would have been a much bigger threat if the USSR and China were **allies.** Nixon made every effort to be friends with China. The USSR, in turn, wanted to be friendly with the United States so that it had an ally against China. Finally, all three countries knew that they could earn money by increasing trade with each other.

Détente in action

In 1968 the Non-Proliferation Treaty, which aimed to stop the spread of nuclear weapons, was signed by the United States, the USSR, and Britain. They agreed that they would not help other countries to build nuclear weapons. Another 59 countries promised not to make them. Unfortunately France, Israel, South Africa, and China refused to sign the treaty. Between 1969 and 1972 the Strategic Arms Limitation Talks (SALT) were held, which resulted in an agreement that became known as SALT I. The United States and the USSR agreed to limit the number of long-range nuclear missiles they would produce over the next five years.

Nixon and Brezhnev sign the SALT I agreement in Moscow in May 1972. The agreement helped to produce friendlier relations between the United States and the USSR.

The most dramatic example of détente in action was a joint U.S.–Soviet space mission in July 1975. Two spacecraft, the Soviet *Soyuz* and the U.S. *Apollo*, docked 155 miles (250 km) above the earth. The two crews shared meals and carried out experiments together. It was a momentous event, and it appeared to point toward a new era of friendliness between the countries. Another breakthrough came on August 1, with the signing of the Helsinki Agreements. Thirty-five countries, including the United States and the USSR, agreed to recognize the 1945 borders of Eastern Europe. They also agreed that all people should have basic human rights: the right to "freedom of thought, religion and belief."

The U.S. astronaut Deke Slayton and the Soviet cosmonaut Alexei Leonov meet each other in space, July 17, 1975.

Relations begin to break down

However, the old distrust between the West and East was still there, and rivalry between the two sides continued. In the Arab–Israeli war of 1973, the Soviets sent aid to the Arabs and the Americans supported the Israelis. Neither side would let inspectors into their country to check the number of nuclear weapons. This left each side suspicious as to whether the other was actually destroying weapons as it had promised.

The Soviets continued to deny their citizens basic human rights. A group of **dissidents** led by Andrei Sakharov, a famous scientist, protested to the government about prison conditions and called for people to be able to travel freely outside the USSR. Sakharov was placed under house arrest. In Afghanistan, a Muslim group, the **Mujaheddin,** rebelled against the government of President Hafizullah Amin. In December 1979, the USSR sent troops into Afghanistan to "restore order." They put a communist government into power that was loyal to Moscow. The Western powers were furious. The invasion brought détente to an end.

Richard Nixon

Richard Nixon was born in California in 1913. He was a **Republican** and became president of the United States in 1969. Nixon was a strong supporter of détente and said that the United States "extended the hand of friendship to the Soviet and Chinese people." He was the first U.S. president to recognize communist China and its leader, Mao Zedong. In 1972 Nixon visited Beijing and Moscow for talks. He took the United States out of Vietnam in 1973, but was forced to resign over the **Watergate** scandal in 1974, and was replaced by Gerald Ford.

Cold War Again

The U.S. president, Jimmy Carter, was angered and dismayed by the Soviet invasion of Afghanistan. He said it was "the greatest threat to world peace since World War II." Relations cooled between the United States and the **USSR** and attitudes hardened once again. Carter immediately stopped U.S. exports of grain to the USSR and **Congress** cancelled the SALT II agreement that had been signed in 1979. This agreement, based on talks that had been going on since 1972, would have further limited the production of nuclear missiles. Instead, Carter increased the size of the U.S. military and allowed the production of a new missile system to go ahead.

In July 1980, the United States and 60 other nations boycotted the Olympic Games in Moscow in protest at the Soviet occupation of Afghanistan. The Soviets retaliated by telling people that there would be CIA agents in the crowd giving away poisoned chewing gum!

The evil empire

On January 21, 1981, Ronald Reagan replaced Carter as U.S. president. Reagan, a **Republican,** was strongly opposed to **communism.** He called the USSR an "evil empire." He wanted to push back communism and win the Cold War battle. Reagan adopted an aggressive stance towards the USSR and its **allies,** and used strong language in his speeches. In 1983, he said that the Cold War was a "struggle between freedom and **totalitarianism,** between what is right and wrong." Under Reagan, **cruise missiles** were placed in NATO countries in Europe, and the United States stopped trading with the USSR.

Nuclear protests

In 1982, it was announced that cruise missiles were to be sited in Britain, at Greenham Common in Berkshire. The news was met with widespread opposition in Britain. On December 12, 1982, over 30,000 women formed a human circle around the Greenham Common air base. The women attached a token from their lives onto the perimeter fence. Many chose to pin up photographs of their children. Other tokens included diapers, anti-war

Supporters of the Campaign for Nuclear Disarmament (CND) protest against cruise missiles outside Greenham Common air base in England, 1983.

poems, and teddy bears. On April 1, 1983, thousands of people protested by joining hands to form a 14-mile (22-kilometer) human chain stretching from the Atomic Weapons Research Establishment at Aldermaston to Greenham Common. Large numbers of women set up a peace camp on the outside of the air base and kept up a daily vigil of protest.

Star Wars

Reagan was frightened that the USSR might launch a nuclear attack on the United States, so in 1983 he introduced the Strategic Defense Initiative (SDI), known as "Star Wars." It was a system that aimed to interrupt foreign missiles, using laser beams fired from satellites in space. It took the arms race almost into the realm of science fiction. Once it was perfected, SDI would provide the United States with the means to survive a first strike attack and enable it to fire missiles back. It would have put the Americans well ahead of the USSR, but was very expensive to develop. Not surprisingly, U.S. defense spending increased from 178 billion dollars in 1981 to 367 billion dollars in 1986. Reagan also sent money to groups fighting left-wing governments in Afghanistan, Nicaragua, El Salvador, and Angola.

Once again there was great tension between East and West. In 1984 the USSR boycotted the Olympic Games, which were held in Los Angeles. It appeared that the two sides would never be friendly again. Few would have imagined the changes that were to occur after 1985.

James Earl (Jimmy) Carter

Carter was born in 1924 in Plains, Georgia. After a career in the U.S. navy, he went back to Georgia and became a peanut farmer. In 1971 Carter, a **Democrat,** was elected governor of Georgia. Six years later, in 1977, he became president of the United States. As president, he persuaded Egypt and Israel to sign a historic peace treaty and was a supporter of human rights. The Afghanistan crisis forced him to take a hard line against the USSR.

President Reagan makes a joke at a press conference to explain the workings of SDI. The SDI helped rekindle the tension between the United States and the USSR.

Enter Mikhail Gorbachev

In 1985 Mikhail Gorbachev became the Soviet leader. He said that the **USSR** had been stagnating since 1982 under the rule of Leonid Brezhnev and that it was time for change. Gorbachev believed in **communism** but thought people should be given more freedom. His ideas were similar to those of Alexander Dubček, who had tried to introduce changes into Czechoslovakia in 1968. Gorbachev announced the twin policies of *perestroika* and *glasnost*. By *perestroika*, Gorbachev meant that he was going to rebuild the Soviet economy so that there would be more goods in the stores at cheaper prices. He said that Soviet factories were expert at building rockets but could not make a decent washing machine. *Glasnost* meant there would be more "openness" and that there would be freedom of speech in the USSR. People would be allowed to discuss politics and criticize the government.

A Soviet SS-20 intermediate range missile being destroyed in 1988.

If the Soviet people were to have a better standard of living, the USSR would need to spend far less on weapons and nuclear missiles. Gorbachev realized that the only way to achieve this was to make friends with the West again and talk about disarmament. He wanted **capitalism** and communism to live peacefully side by side.

On November 21, 1985, Gorbachev met President Ronald Reagan in Geneva. The two men talked for six hours about the Cold War and how the West and East could make a fresh start. Afterward, Gorbachev said that the two men had got on well and the world had become a safer place. People in the West warmed to the Soviet leader. They liked his honesty and cheerful personality. Slowly, trust was replacing mistrust.

In October 1986, the two **superpower** leaders met again in Reykjavik, Iceland. They agreed to scrap some of their nuclear missiles but then Gorbachev said he wanted Reagan to stop the Strategic Defense Initiative ("Star Wars") program. Reagan refused, but invited Gorbachev to visit the United States at a later date. Gorbachev remained positive and invited Western leaders to visit the USSR. In March 1987, the people of Moscow gave Margaret Thatcher, the British prime minister, an enthusiastic welcome.

The breakthrough in arms reduction finally came at a summit meeting in Washington, D.C. in December 1987 when Reagan and Gorbachev signed the Intermediate Nuclear Forces Treaty. Both sides agreed to destroy all missiles that had a range of between 310 and 3,441 miles (500 and 5,550 km). To make sure that they were doing as they promised, teams of inspectors were allowed to count the number of missiles. It looked as though the Cold War was coming to an end.

Reagan visited Moscow in June 1988, where he praised Gorbachev's attitude, saying that their talks had made "huge breaches in the walls of the Cold War fortress." And this was from a man who five years before had called the USSR "an evil empire." In December 1988, Gorbachev told the **United Nations (UN)** that he would cut the Soviet army by ten percent, or 500,000 soldiers.

Gorbachev's efforts to end the Cold War made him very popular in the West. The newspapers called it "Gorby Mania." But in the **satellite** countries of Eastern Europe, people saw a chance to break free from the USSR. The year 1989 was to see dramatic changes in Eastern Europe.

Mikhail and Raisa Gorbachev leaving a polling station after voting in a local election in Moscow, March 18, 1990.

Raisa Gorbachev

Raisa Maximovna Titorenko was the daughter of a railway worker. Born in 1932, she was a brilliant student. She gained a place at Moscow University, where she met Mikhail Gorbachev. They married in 1955. When her husband became the Soviet leader, Raisa gave him all the support she could. He nicknamed her "My General" and said that he always asked for her views before making a decision. Raisa was known for her warmth and confidence, and was always immaculately dressed. The heavy workload of her husband caused her to worry. "His worries are also my worries," she said. In August 1991, Raisa suffered a stroke, followed by a heart attack in 1993. The "first lady of Soviet chic" died of leukemia in Sept 1999, at the age of 67.

1989: Year of Revolutions

The countries of Eastern Europe had been under the control of the **USSR** since 1945. Attempts to break free, for instance in Hungary (1956) and Czechoslovakia (1968), had been crushed by the Soviet army. In March 1989, Mikhail Gorbachev said that the USSR would never again use force to impose its will on the countries of Eastern Europe. He also said that he would begin to withdraw Soviet troops from Eastern Europe, giving people the freedom to choose the kind of government they wanted.

The communist leaders of Eastern European countries were dismayed, but the ordinary people sensed that the time was right to end **communism** and break away from the USSR. People were tired of communism: it had failed to bring them a comfortable standard of living and did not allow basic human rights. They looked with envy at the wealth and freedoms of the **democratic** countries in the West. By the end of 1989, communism had completely collapsed in Eastern Europe. It was an amazing turnaround.

A man smashes down the Berlin Wall in November 1989. The bemused guards can only stand and watch. The Wall had been a hated symbol of the Cold War for 28 years.

In May, the Hungarian government took down the barbed-wire fence that bordered noncommunist Austria. Thousands of East Germans traveled to Hungary, crossed into Austria and went on into West Germany. There was nothing anyone could do to stop them. In Poland, which had been the first Soviet **satellite** to defy Moscow in the early 1980s, the trade union Solidarity beat the communists in elections. The Solidarity leader, Lech Walesa, later became president of a democratic country.

The Berlin Wall comes down

The East German leader, Erich Honecker, wanted to hold on to power, but was very unpopular. On October 7, Gorbachev visited East Berlin and told the people "to take democracy if they wanted it." On October 9, there was a mass march of 100,000 people in the East German city of Leipzig, calling for elections.

The momentum was for change. On October 18, Honecker was forced to resign and was replaced by Egon Krenz, a moderate communist. Krenz said that people were free to travel to the West if they wanted. The East Germans took this to mean that the Berlin Wall had been opened. On the night of November 9, thousands of people flocked to the Wall and they demanded to be let through to West Berlin. As they walked through the checkpoint, the confused border guards could only stand and watch. There were wild scenes of rejoicing. Hundreds climbed onto the Wall and began to hack it to pieces. Berlin was no longer a divided city.

On November 10 the communist leader in Bulgaria resigned. One week later, on November 17, in Prague, Czechoslovakia, police brutally beat up people who were protesting against the communist government. There followed a week of massive demonstrations in which people called for democracy. On November 24, the government resigned. There was hardly any bloodshed, so the overthrow of the communist regime became known as the "Velvet Revolution." Vaclav Havel, a famous playwright who had long opposed communism, became the new president of a democratic Czechoslovakia. Finally, in December communism came to a violent end in Romania.

The body of Nicolae Ceausescu, as shown on Romanian television. The Romanian people were pleased to see his downfall.

Death of a tyrant

Nicolae Ceausescu became the leader of Romania in 1967. He refused to be dominated by Moscow. He visited the United States in 1972 and Britain in 1978. Little did the people of Western Europe realize at the time what a tyrant they were befriending. Anyone who dared to criticize Ceausescu was arrested by the Securitate (secret police), imprisoned, and tortured. On December 17, 1989, there was a demonstration against Ceausescu in the town of Timisoara. People called out, "We want bread" and "Down with Ceausescu." The secret police opened fire and killed thousands of people. On December 22, Ceausescu called a public meeting in Bucharest to show the people that he was in control. The crowd booed him and threw stones. The next day he and his wife fled Bucharest in a helicopter. The Ceausescus were soon caught by the army, put on trial, and on December 25, executed by firing squad.

The End of the Cold War

On a stormy morning on December 2, 1989, U.S. President George H. W. Bush and the Soviet leader Mikhail Gorbachev met on board the *Maxim Gorky*, a Soviet warship, off the coast of Malta. They formally announced that the Cold War was over. Further talks on reducing nuclear weapons were to be held, and trade links between the United States and the **USSR** strengthened. In 1991 the Strategic Arms Reduction Treaty (START) was signed, which reduced the number of Soviet nuclear missiles by 5,000 and U.S. ones by 3,500.

> *I do not regard the end of the Cold War as a victory for one side. The end of the Cold War is our common victory.*
>
> Mikhail Gorbachev

The breakup of the USSR

By 1990, Gorbachev had become very unpopular in the USSR. *Perestroika* was not working. Prices were high and ordinary goods were in short supply. People still had to stand in line for hours to buy food. Some politicians inside the **Communist** Party did not like the changes at all, while others thought things were not changing fast enough. Gorbachev was openly criticized and heckled when he spoke in public. The republics that made up the USSR demanded their independence.

People in Moscow plead with a tank driver not to support the coup against Gorbachev in August 1991.

On August 19, 1991, a group of hard-line communists tried to overthrow Gorbachev. At the time, Mikhail and Raisa Gorbachev were on vacation in the Crimea. Members of the **KGB** put them under house arrest. In Moscow, the **coup** leaders sent tanks onto the streets, but ordinary people confronted the soldiers and asked them to leave. Boris Yeltsin, the president of Russia, called for Gorbachev to be released. On August 21, the leaders of the coup gave themselves up and were imprisoned. Gorbachev returned to Moscow looking tired and anxious.

Yeltsin made it clear that he had been responsible for saving Gorbachev. Yeltsin wanted to see the end of communism, so he forced Gorbachev to ban the Communist Party. By December 1991, the USSR had broken up. All of its fifteen

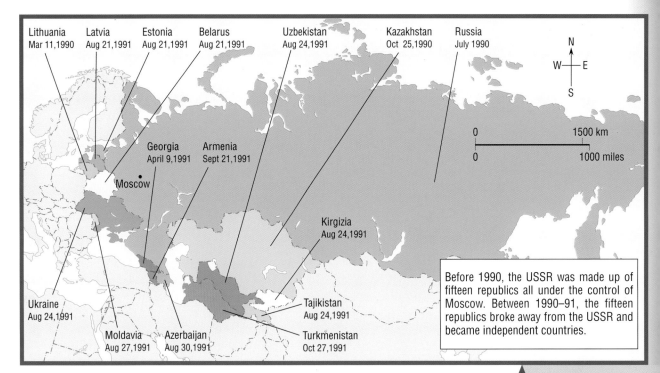

Lithuania
Mar 11,1990

Latvia
Aug 21,1991

Estonia
Aug 21,1991

Belarus
Aug 21,1991

Uzbekistan
Aug 24,1991

Kazakhstan
Oct 25,1990

Russia
July 1990

Georgia
April 9,1991

Armenia
Sept 21,1991

Moscow

Kirgizia
Aug 24,1991

Ukraine
Aug 24,1991

Moldavia
Aug 27,1991

Azerbaijan
Aug 30,1991

Tajikistan
Aug 24,1991

Turkmenistan
Oct 27,1991

Before 1990, the USSR was made up of fifteen republics all under the control of Moscow. Between 1990–91, the fifteen republics broke away from the USSR and became independent countries.

member republics had declared themselves independent. On December 25, Gorbachev announced his resignation as Soviet president. As he spoke, the red flag with the hammer and sickle was lowered over the Kremlin. As Russia was the most powerful republic of the old USSR, its president, Yeltsin, was now in control of the nuclear weapons.

The world since the Cold War

Despite the ending of the Cold War, the world is not free of nuclear weapons. The United States, Russia, Britain, and France still possess long-range missiles. In 1998, both India and Pakistan carried out nuclear tests. So, though less likely than during the Cold War years, the possibility of a **nuclear war** is still with us.

After the Berlin Wall came down, West and East Germany became one country again, but problems remain. East Germans have their freedom and can vote in free elections, but people in the old West Germany are critical of how much taxpayers' money has been spent on the East; people in the East see themselves as poor relations. It has been harder to mold the two Germanys into one nation than people imagined.

In the old communist countries, **democracy** has not brought an end to poverty. The Czech Republic, Hungary, Poland, and Romania want to be full members of the **European Union (EU).** This will bring them into a family of **democratic** nations and enable them to build up trading links.

So the Cold War's demise has not brought a perfect world, but at least the cloud of extreme mistrust, suspicion, and paranoia between the East and West has been lifted. It remains to be seen what the future holds.

This map shows the rapid breakup of the USSR, 1990–91. The date of each republic's independence is shown after its name.

Cold War Timeline

	KEY EVENTS	ARMS RACE and SPACE RACE	U.S. PRESIDENTS	SOVIET LEADERS
1945	Yalta and Potsdam conferences, 1945 Churchill's "Iron Curtain" speech, 1946 Truman Doctrine and Marshall Plan, 1947 Berlin blockade and airlift, 1948–49 NATO formed, 1949	U.S. drops atomic bombs on Hiroshima and Nagasaki, Japan, 1945 USSR explodes an atomic bomb, 1949	Harry S. Truman (1945–53)	Josef Stalin [died 1953]
1950	Korean War, 1950–53	First hydrogen bomb (United States), 1952		
1955	Warsaw Pact formed, 1955 Revolt in Hungary against the USSR, 1956	Sputnik 1—first satellite (USSR), 1957	Dwight D. Eisenhower (1953–61)	Nikita Krushchev (1953–64)
1960	U–2 spy plane crisis, 1960 Berlin Wall goes up, 1961 Cuban Missile Crisis, 1962 Kennedy visits Berlin, 1963	Yuri Gagarin (USSR) orbits Earth, 1961 Test Ban Treaty, 1963	John F. Kennedy (1961–63)	
1965	Operation Rolling Thunder (Vietnam), 1965 Prague Spring; start of détente, 1968	Non-Proliferation Treaty, 1968 First men on the moon (United States), 1969	Lyndon B. Johnson (1963–69)	Leonid Brezhnev (1964–82)
1970	United States pulls troops out of Vietnam, 1973	SALT I, 1972	Richard M. Nixon (1969–74)	
1975	Helsinki agreement, 1975	Joint U.S./Soviet space mission, 1975	Gerald Ford (1974–77)	
1980	USSR invades Afghanistan; end of détente, 1979 United States boycotts Moscow Olympics, 1980	SALT II, 1979 (canceled 1980) SDI (Star Wars) announced by United States, 1983	Jimmy Carter (1977–81)	Yuri Andropov (1982–84) Konstantin Chernenko (1984–85)
1985	USSR boycotts Los Angeles Olympics, 1984 Reykjavik summit, 1986 Reagan visits Moscow, 1988		Ronald Reagan (1981–89)	Mikhail Gorbachev (1985–91)
1990	Berlin Wall comes down; end of Cold War, 1989 Breakup of the USSR, 1990		George H. W. Bush (1989–93)	

Map of the Cold War Hot Spots

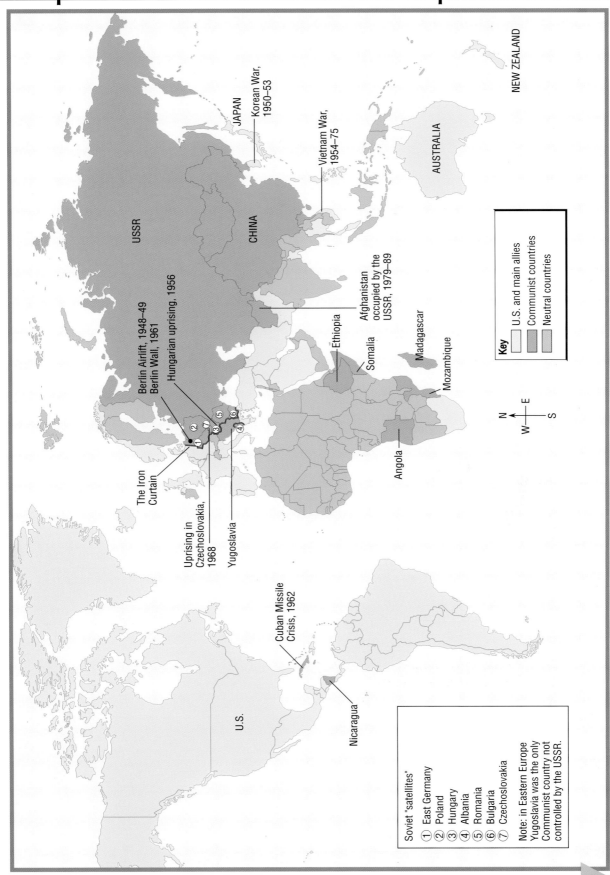

NEW ZEALAND

JAPAN

Korean War, 1950–53

Vietnam War, 1954–75

AUSTRALIA

USSR

CHINA

Afghanistan occupied by the USSR, 1979–89

Berlin Airlift, 1948—49
Berlin Wall, 1961

Hungarian uprising, 1956

Ethiopia

Somalia

Madagascar

Mozambique

Angola

The Iron Curtain

Uprising in Czechoslovakia, 1968

Yugoslavia

Key

U.S. and main allies
Communist countries
Neutral countries

N
W — E
S

Cuban Missile Crisis, 1962

U.S.

Nicaragua

Soviet "satellites"
① East Germany
② Poland
③ Hungary
④ Albania
⑤ Romania
⑥ Bulgaria
⑦ Czechoslovakia

Note: in Eastern Europe Yugoslavia was the only Communist country not controlled by the USSR.

More Books to Read

Nonfiction

Cheney, Glenn Alan. *Nuclear Proliferation: The Problems and Possibilities.* Danbury, Conn.: Franklin Watts, Inc., 1999.

Grant, R.G. *The Berlin Wall.* Austin, Tex.: Raintree Steck-Vaughn, 1998.

Kallen, Stuart A. *Gorbachev/Yeltsin: The Fall of Communism.* Edina, Minn.:ABDO, 1992.

Kelly, Nigel. *The Fall of the Berlin Wall.* Chicago: Heinemann Library, 2000.

Kelly, Nigel. *The Moon Landing.* Chicago: Heinemann Library, 2000.

Sherrow, Victoria. *Joseph McCarthy and the Cold War.* Woodbridge, Conn.: Blackbirch Press, 1998.

Shuter, Jane. *Russia and the USSR.* Chicago: Heinemann Library, 1996.

Stein, Conrad R. *The Great Red Scare.* Columbus, Ohio: Silver Burdett Press, 1997.

Warren, James A. *Cold War: The American Crusade Against the Soviet Union & World Communism.* Fairfield, N.J.: Lothrop, Lee & Shepard Books, 1996.

Fiction

Degens, T. *Freya on the Wall.* New York: Harcourt Trade Publishers, 1997.

Schneider, Peter. *The Wall Jumper: A Berlin Story.* Chicago: University of Chicago Press, 1998.

Glossary

allies countries who fight together for a common purpose

attorney general chief officer of the law in the United States who heads the Department of Justice

Bolshevik Party political party led by Vladimir Lenin that seized control of Russia in 1917

capitalism system which uses private wealth to produce goods

censoring when a government checks newspapers, television programs, and movies and removes material it does not want published

communism system in which the state owns all means of wealth production

Congress law-making body of the United States, made up of the House of Representatives and the Senate

conventional weapons non-nuclear weapons

coup takeover of a country by a small group, usually by violent means

cruise missiles long-range U.S. nuclear missiles

defectors people who desert a country

democracy government by elected representatives

Democratic Party one of the two main political parties in the United States; generally supports more government presence in people's lives

détente the relaxing of tension between the East and West

dissidents people who disagree strongly with the policies of a government

European Union (EU) group of European countries that trades freely with each other and shares a common defense policy

guerrillas small groups of soldiers who spring surprise attacks on the enemy

intelligence gathering of secret military information by spies

KGB Soviet secret police; its full name in Russian is the *Komitet Gosudarstvennoy Bezopasnosti*, which means "Committee for State Security"

Mujaheddin Muslim guerrilla fighters in Afghanistan who believe that the country should be ruled according to strict Muslim religious rules

Nazi led by Adolf Hitler, the Nazis (National Socialist Workers' Party) controlled Germany from 1933–45

nuclear warfare war using either atomic bombs or hydrogen bombs

pacifist person who does not believe in fighting wars

propaganda information to make people believe certain ideas or viewpoints

Quakers members of the Society of Friends, a religious group that believes in pacifism

radiation sickness illnesses caused by the fallout from a nuclear explosion

RAF British Royal Air Force

rationing when the supply of food is limited and controlled

Red Army army of the USSR

Republican Party one of the two main political parties in the United States, it favors big business and is against the government interfering in people's lives

Russian Civil War war fought between the Reds (communists) and Whites (supporters of Czar Nicholas II) from 1918 to 1921; it was won by the Reds

Russian Revolution communist seizure of power in Russia in 1917

satellite country that is dominated by a larger, more powerful country

secretary of state person in the U.S. government who is responsible for foreign affairs

second front opening of another fighting front in Western Europe during World War II when Britain and the United States invaded France on June 6, 1944. The first front was opened in 1941, when Nazi Germany invaded the USSR.

superpower name for the United States and the USSR, who emerged from World War II as the two most powerful countries in the world

totalitarian when one political party rules a country, banning other political parties and free speech

Union of Soviet Socialist Republics (USSR) first created in 1923 by the union of four republics: Russia, the Ukraine, Belarus, and the Caucasus. It grew to include fifteen communist republics. It broke up in 1991.

United Nations (UN) association of countries formed after World War II to work for world peace

USAF United States Air Force

Vietcong communist guerrilla who fought the Americans in South Vietnam

Vietminh shortened name for the League for the Independence of Vietnam, formed in 1941 by Ho Chi Minh

Watergate biggest political scandal in U.S. history, brought about when five men hired by the Republican Party broke into the Watergate complex in Washington D.C., in 1972, the headquarters of the Democratic Party. The scandal led to the resignation of President Richard Nixon in 1974.

Index